FIND IT! CANADA

A Search and Find Activity Book

by Jeff Sinclair

Scholastic Canada Ltd.

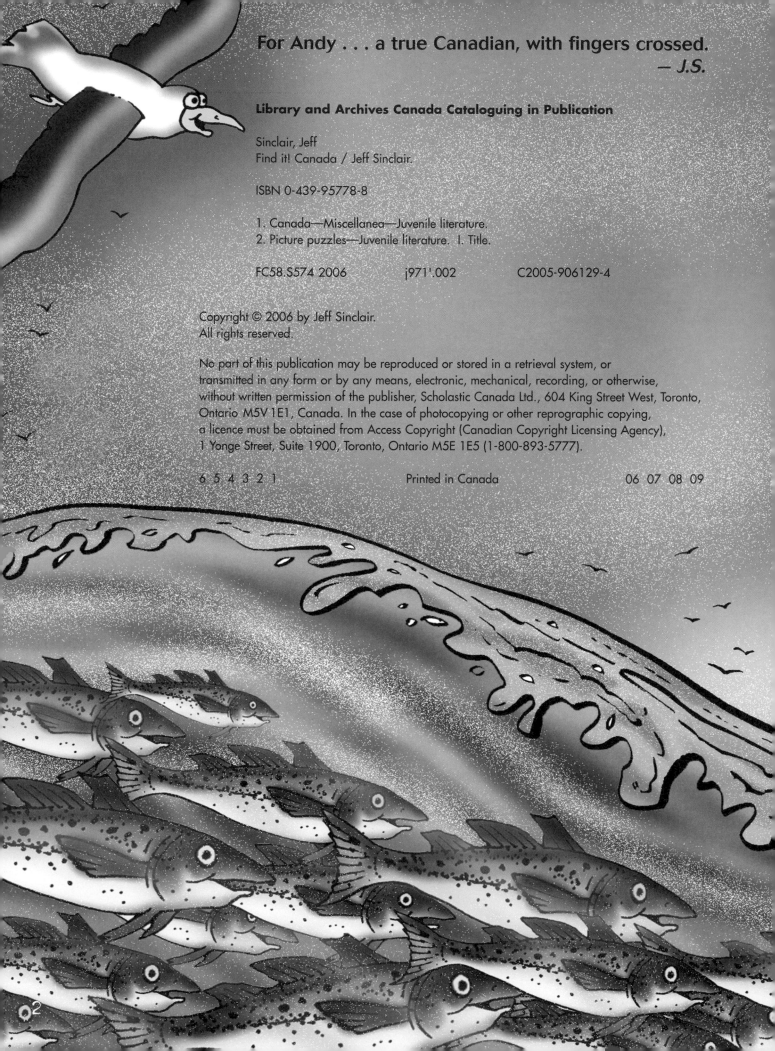

For Andy . . . a true Canadian, with fingers crossed.
— J.S.

Library and Archives Canada Cataloguing in Publication

Sinclair, Jeff
Find it! Canada / Jeff Sinclair.

ISBN 0-439-95778-8

1. Canada—Miscellanea—Juvenile literature.
2. Picture puzzles—Juvenile literature. I. Title.

FC58.S574 2006   j971'.002   C2005-906129-4

6 5 4 3 2 1   Printed in Canada   06 07 08 09

CANADA . . . the more you look, the more you FIND!

There are so many things to see and do in Canada, our home and native land, that it's hard to find a place to start. Well, look no further than these pages. They're a colourful, cross-country kaleidoscope of Canadian sights and scenes.

Each double-page spread is chock full of fun and friendly Canadian items and icons to spot. Some are easy to see and some are hiding here and there.

So come join the fun and prepare to be dazzled. If you can't find an item, try not to get frazzled!

Barky Beaver's BONUS Challenge

BONUS! Barky has added a tough and tricky twist to every spread in the book. He challenges you to find ONE Canadian item that doesn't belong in each Canadian scene. Turn to page 32 to fill in the answers, then solve a hidden message!

3

THE WONDERFUL WEST COAST

The rain has stopped and the sun is shining on Vancouver in beautiful British Columbia. Take a leisurely look around this cool Canadian city and see what you can find.

STANLEY PARK

TO UBC

GRANVILLE ISLAND

1. a seagull with a clam
2. 2 university signs
3. a Chinese lantern
4. a sasquatch footprint
5. the Gastown Steam Clock
6. the provincial flag
7. 2 beluga whales
8. 13 yellow raincoats
9. 20 umbrellas
10. I ♥ BC bumper sticker
11. the SkyTrain
12. Ogopogo
13. 3 black bears
14. a wild salmon
15. a beaver totem
16. a truckload of V-chips (invented in BC!)
17. a Chinese dragon
18. 6 eagle feathers
19. a sleepy Steller's jay
20. a dedicated jogger

GOLF

Mall Madness

West Edmonton Mall has it all!
From rockin' roller coasters to awesome aquatic
adventures, it's the Greatest Indoor Show on Earth.
You'll need a keen eye to spot all the attractions.
Have fun!

1. a tourist's camera
2. s-s-s-snow
3. a periscope
4. a scary shark
5. a fish out of water
6. a performing sea lion
7. the Alberta flag
8. 5 palm trees
9. a red golf ball
10. a purse
11. a butterfly
12. 2 chubby cacti
13. 6 stray balloons
14. a hockey stick
15. a treasure chest
16. a pair of sunglasses
17. Sharky the mascot
18. a high-diving penguin
19. a sea turtle
20. a pink seashell

There's GOLD in them thar hills! But gold's not the only precious item in the Yukon Territory. Pick up a shovel and dig around for lots of lost and legendary items along the Chilkoot Trail.

1. 6 bags of gold dust
2. an ice age stone knife
3. 3 sets of elk horns
4. 5 clumps of fireweed
5. a mine shaft
6. 6 Yukon Gold potatoes
7. a missing mitten
8. Mount Logan
9. a pick and shovel
10. the Yukon flag
11. cougar tracks
12. a handsaw
13. a black spruce
14. a gold ring
15. 6 small gold pans
16. a radical raven
17. a compass
18. a white horse
19. a broken lantern
20. 8 grizzly claws

Summer in the City

COTTAGE COUNTRY

1. a jumbo jet
2. 21 orange traffic cones
3. a streetcar named King
4. a happy hippo
5. a huge Leaf
6. 2 balloons
7. a stretch limo
8. a TTC subway train
9. a satellite dish
10. 2 blue jays
11. 2 hockey sticks
12. big smoke
13. 2 ferries
14. 3 streetlights out
15. a Canada goose feather
16. a raptor
17. 2 domes
18. a beach ball
19. snow left over from March
20. a roller coaster

From high atop the CN Tower, gaze out across the city of Toronto. Canada's most massive metropolis is a multicultural marvel.

From the ACC to the TTC, search for a multitude of things that make Toronto terrific!

At the Lake

Hit the beach on Lake Winnipeg as summer vacation goes to full throttle. Get in the swim of things and find all the fun and fascinating items that make Grand Beach so grand!

1. a lunging muskie
2. an ice cream cone
3. a red and yellow beach ball
4. 6 snorkels
5. a lost wallet
6. the Manitoba flag
7. a buffalo
8. 20 herring gulls
9. 3 pink frisbees
10. a swim fin
11. a boom box
12. a tennis ball
13. a wristwatch
14. 5 sandwiches
15. a side of fries
16. 4 toonies
17. 6 blue coolers
18. a flip-flop
19. a fishing rod
20. spilled sunscreen lotion

Hitch a ride on a racing chuck wagon and bust a bronco at the rowdiest rodeo on the face of the Earth. Then mosey on over to the midway and find some cool Canadian country items.

1. 6 bales of hay
2. 2 orders of fries
3. a spur
4. spilled pop
5. a camcorder
6. a lasso
7. 4 bolo ties
8. 1 ride ticket
9. 10 hamburgers
10. 8 blue jay feathers
11. 14 cowboy hats
12. a buckin' bronco
13. a buffalo skull
14. 3 little pigs
15. the Saddledome
16. 6 hot dogs
17. a bald eagle feather
18. a bugle
19. an award winner
20. a striped straw

The tide has turned on the salty shores of Newfoundland. Search the harbour above and below the waterline to seek out what makes this Atlantic island so awesome. Dive in and get hooked!

LUCKY II

Fascinating Fortress LOUISBOURG

Step through the gate and back in time to 1745, when this fortified town was a thriving community in what is now Nova Scotia.

While you're getting a glimpse of one of Canada's greatest heritage sites, search around for assorted items of the past.

1. 2 anchors
2. a lock and key
3. 6 oyster shells
4. a red rooster
5. 14 loaves of fresh bread
6. a pewter bowl and spoon
7. a pair of spectacles
8. 6 French silver coins
9. mayflowers
10. a pile of musket shot
11. dried codfish
12. a clay tobacco pipe
13. 3 goose eggs
14. a cannonball
15. a violin
16. 2 cabbage plants
17. a soldier's lost knife
18. an earring
19. 3 pails
20. a broken wagon wheel

Glories of the Fall

The maples, now clad in their brightest display,
Filter sunbeams that sparkle across Georgian Bay.
The cool air of autumn breathes deep in the woods
As animals scurry to store winter goods.
  Look about and you may see
  Something hidden beneath a tree!

1. a solitary snail
2. a crow's nest
3. a 4-point buck
4. a bearpaw print
5. a not-so-busy beaver
6. 10 butterflies
7. 6 ladybugs
8. 3 chickadees
9. 1 red fish egg
10. 2 dragonflies
11. a rascally rabbit
12. 4 wildflowers
13. 2 BIG mosquitoes
14. a moose
15. a lost flashlight
16. a cheeky chipmunk
17. a raven
18. 4 earthworms
19. 2 raccoon tails
20. a styrofoam cup

Land of the Midnight Sun

1. 5 inuksuks
2. 14 polar bear tracks
3. an iced tea
4. a polar pileup
5. a lazy lemming
6. a whalebone needle
7. an Inuit drum
8. 12 walrus tusks
9. the aurora borealis
10. a lichen-covered rock
11. caribou-hoo
12. a pile of clams
13. an orca
14. a fishing hook
15. 2 belugas
16. 6 arctic bumblebees
17. 3 blueberry popsicles
18. an ice cube
19. a hunting harpoon
20. a snowflake

Put on your warmest parka and that new pair of mukluks
to cross the freshly fallen snow on a frigid Nunavut night.
Check out the inhabitants and take in all the sights —
There's lots to find, including the astounding northern lights!

Where's a cool place to be?
Quebec City in February.
Come and give Bonhomme a hand
searching through the snow for some
far-out and f-f-f-frosty items.
Carnaval de Québec – c'est magnifique!

1. a square snowflake
2. the Quebec flag
3. a toboggan
4. snowshoe tracks
5. a cold Canadian maple leaf
6. an oversized hockey puck
7. a snow cone
8. an icy swan
9. a bottle of maple syrup
10. an accordion
11. 3 orders of poutine
12. a lost leash
13. a canoe
14. 4 red and white tuques
15. a chickadee
16. a frozen fleur-de-lys
17. a cool haircut
18. a pink scarf
19. a chateau
20. 2 snowmen with top hats

Flat Out Fun!

1. a pitchfork
2. a silo
3. 9 hefty hogs
4. 3 prairie chickens
5. 6 Canada geese
6. a bottle of canola oil
7. a red turnip beetle
8. a western red lily
9. a meadowlark
10. 10 prairie chicken eggs
11. 2 tractor nuts and a bolt
12. a bag of sunflower seeds
13. a bird on a wire
14. a fishing fly
15. the Saskatchewan flag
16. 5 gopher holes
17. 2 POOLs
18. a bad sunburn
19. a goose feather
20. a gusher

Shade your eyes in the Land of the Living Skies — with wheat fields as far as the eye can see and oil derricks churning up liquid gold, Saskatchewan shines! Find all the items and you'll be outstanding in your field!

Pastoral P.E.I.

1. 3 distant sailboats
2. a shining searchlight
3. a hunting heron
4. Petey Potato and family
5. 30 soaring seagulls
6. 3 standing seagulls
7. 3 green gables
8. an orange buoy
9. a red-winged blackbird
10. a basket of blueberries
11. a banded bird
12. a bald eagle
13. a solo spud
14. 3 solitary sandpipers
15. a hermit crab
16. a minnow on the menu
17. 3 little lobsters
18. 3 lovely lady's slippers
19. a floating bobber
20. a fishing net

30

As you journey across Confederation Bridge, the island "cradled by the waves" unfolds its beauty before you. Stop by to visit Anne, or take the road less travelled to the sandy shore. Wherever you go, Prince Edward Island is full of surprises!

Barky Beaver's BONUS Challenge

Hidden in each Canadian scene in this book is something that does not belong. If you want a challenge, SEARCH through every spread to FIND it, and print its name here. Then, using only the letters in the circles, rearrange them below to reveal an all-Canadian hidden message!

Page 4-5 _ Ⓞ _ H _ _ M E

Page 6-7 _ A P _ ◯ S _ P

Page 8-9 L _ B S _ _ Ⓡ

Page 10-11 S _ ◯ Q U _ _ C H

Page 12-13 _ E ◯ L

Page 14-15 P _ F _ ◯ N

Page 16-17 S ◯ _ K E

Page 18-19 _ I Ⓖ _ T H _ _ S E

Page 20-21 B ◯ _ C K _ E Ⓡ _ Y

Page 22-23 S T A _ Ⓕ _ _ H

Page 24-25 H _ M M _ _ _ B _ _ Ⓓ

Page 26-27 C _ _ T Ⓞ _ E R

Page 28-29 _ N ◯ K _ U K

Page 30-31 _ O O _ Ⓔ

Hidden Message:

◯ ◯ ◯ ◯ ◯ ◯ ◯ ◯ ◯ ◯ ◯ ◯ ◯ ◯ ◯ !